I0511321

Niagara-on-the-Lake Ontario Book 3 in Colour Photos, Saving Our History One Photo at a Time

Photography
by Barbara Raué
2015

Series Name:
Cruising Ontario

Book 104: Niagara-on-the-Lake Book 3

Cover photo: 132 Prideaux Street, see Page 35

Series Name: Cruising Ontario
Saving Our History One Photo at a Time
in colour photos

Other Books by Barbara Raue

Coins of Gold

Arrows, Indians and Love

The Life and Times of Barbara
Volume 1: Inventions That Have Enhanced My Life
Volume 2: Entertainment That I Have Enjoyed
Volume 3: East Coast Trips
Volume 4: Olympics Have Always Intrigued Me
Volume 5: Wonders of the World
Volume 6: Caribbean Cruises We Have Enjoyed
Volume 7: Animals
Volume 8: Storms and Other Major Disasters in My Lifetime
Volume 9: Wars, Terrorist Attacks and Major Disasters

The Cromwell Family Book

Laura Secord Discovered

Daddy Where Are You?

Visit Barbara's website to view all of her books
http://barbararaue.ca

The Fortified Mouth of the Niagara River

The St. Lawrence and Great Lakes system was the most efficient route to the interior of the continent of North America. Large waterways allowed for substantial sailing vessels to trade and maintain contact with Native allies from Montreal to the Mississippi with minimal portages and transshipment in smaller boats. The one great obstacle along the chain of waterways was Niagara Falls whose dramatic height required some control of the land to allow for a portage around the escarpment and the falls to the lakes beyond. The strategic importance of this area led to the construction of several forts at the mouth of the river in an attempt to control this critical water route.

Table of Contents

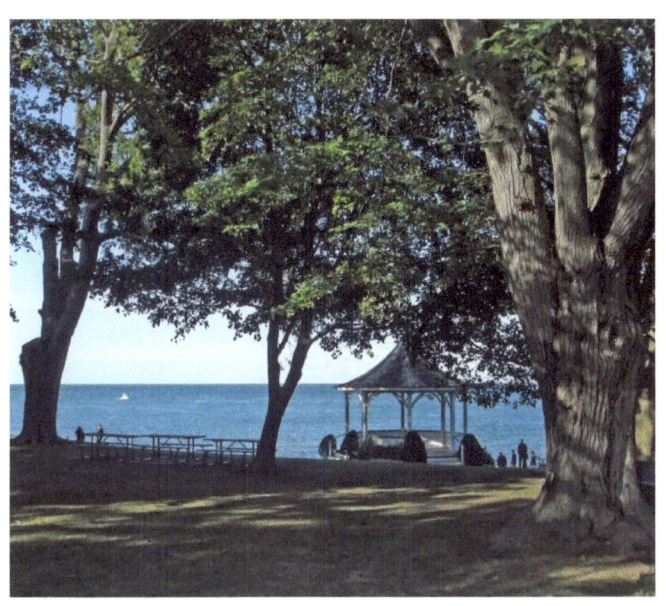

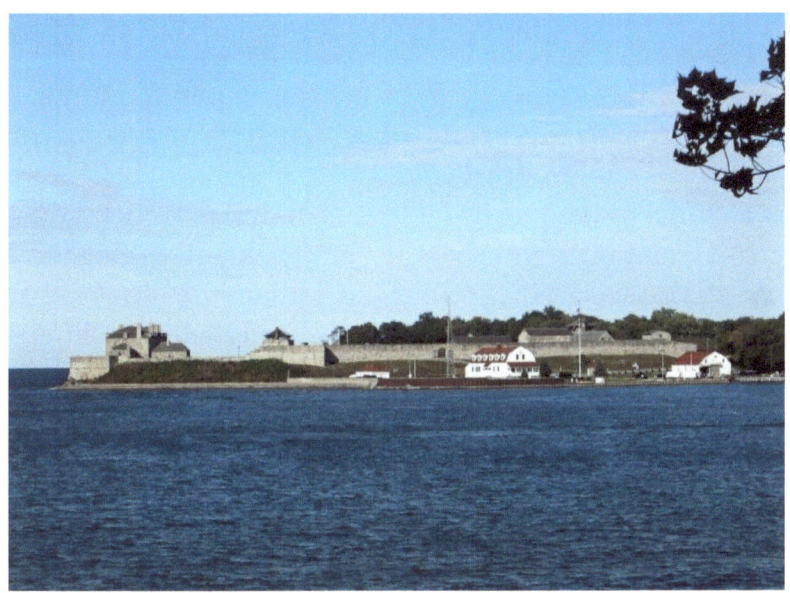

American Fort Niagara

Fort Niagara

Fort Niagara is a fortification originally built to protect the interests of New France in North America. It is located near Youngstown, New York, on the eastern bank of the Niagara River at its mouth, on Lake Ontario.

René-Robert Cavelier, Sieur de la Salle built the first French structure, called Fort Conti, in 1678. In 1687, the Governor of New France, the Marquis de Denonville, constructed a new fort, a small wooden complex, at the former site of Fort Conti. He named it Fort Denonville and posted a hundred men there. The winter weather and disease was severe, and all but twelve perished by the time a relief force returned from Montreal. It was decided in September 1688 to abandon the post and the stockade was pulled down. In 1726, the first stone structure, a two storey building was constructed on the same site. It was a critical post for fur trade and defensive works against the Iroquois.

The name used today, "The French Castle" was not used until the 19th Century. The fort was expanded to its present size in 1755 due to increased tensions between French and British colonial interests.

The fort played a significant part in the French and Indian War, and suffered the only European-style siege in North America in 1759. It fell to the British in a nineteen day siege in July 1759, called the Battle of Fort Niagara. The French relief force sent for the besieged garrison was ambushed at the Battle of La Belle Famille, and the commander of the post, Francois Pouchot, surrendered the fort to the British commander, Sir William Johnson, who initially led the New York Militia. The Irish-born Johnson was not the original commander of the expedition, but became its leader when General Prideaux literally lost his head, stepping in front of a mortar being test-fired during the siege. The fort remained in British hands for the next thirty-seven years.

Fort Niagara served as the Loyalist base in New York during the American Revolutionary War for Colonel John Butler and his Butler's Rangers, a Tory militia in the command of the British Army. Though Fort Niagara was ceded to the United States after the Treaty of Paris ended the American War of Independence in 1783, the region remained effectively under British control for thirteen years. In the interim, United Empire Loyalists fleeing persecution in the new United States of America were given land grants, typically 200 acres (81 hectares) per inhabitant in Upper Canada, and some were sustained in the early years partly by aid from the military stores of the fort. Only after signing of the Jay Treaty did American forces occupy the fort in 1796. The Niagara River now marked the boundary between the British colony and the United States. Cannons from the American fort easily commanded the mouth of the river.

The fort was engaged in several artillery duels in 1812 and was severely damaged during the War of 1812. It was the base of American operations for the Battle of Fort George.

The British captured Fort Niagara on the night of December 19, 1813. British forces relinquished it to the United States with the Treaty of Ghent. It has remained in U.S. custody ever since.

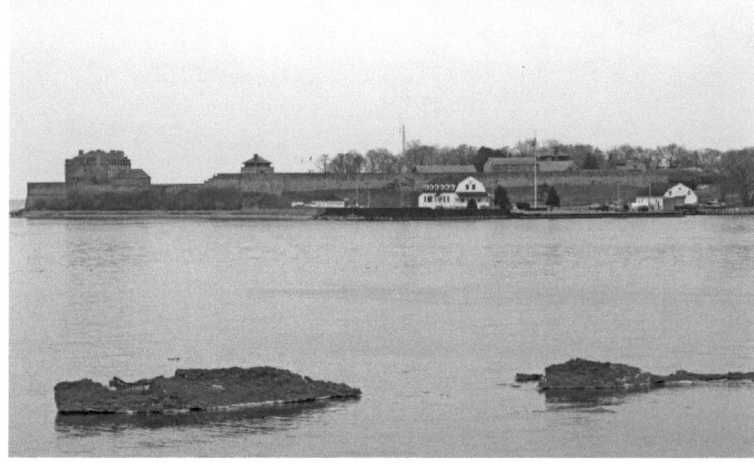

The name "Old Fort Niagara" which is associated with the fort today does not refer to its age but to distinguish the colonial-era fortress from its more modern namesake. The post-Civil War era saw the building of "New Fort Niagara" outside the original walls of the fort. Following the Civil War, masonry forts were abandoned for the style of military camp we now know (masonry fared poorly under bombardment). The newer Fort Niagara contained a thousand-yard rifle range, access to rail lines, and access to large industrial areas (Niagara Falls and Buffalo). Fort Niagara was used to train troops for the Spanish-American War and World War I and during World War II as an induction center and later a Prisoner of War camp for 1,200 German soldiers captured in North Africa. After World War II, the fort served as emergency housing for returning veterans. During the Korean War, the fort was used for the headquarters for anti-aircraft artillery and later Nike missiles. The U.S. Army officially deactivated Fort Niagara in 1963. Military presence on the site continues with the United States Coast Guard still operating at "The Bottoms" making Fort Niagara one of the longest continuously run military bases in the United States.

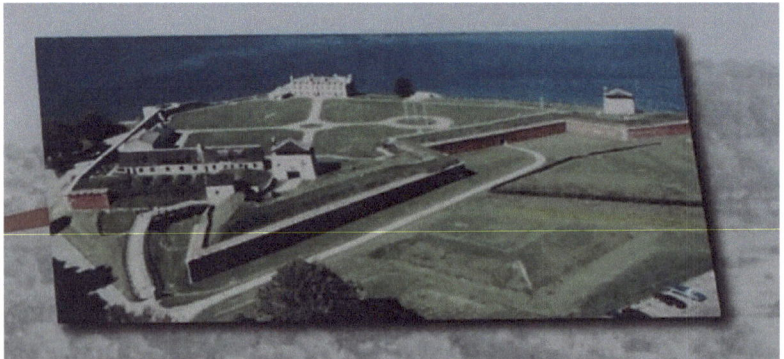

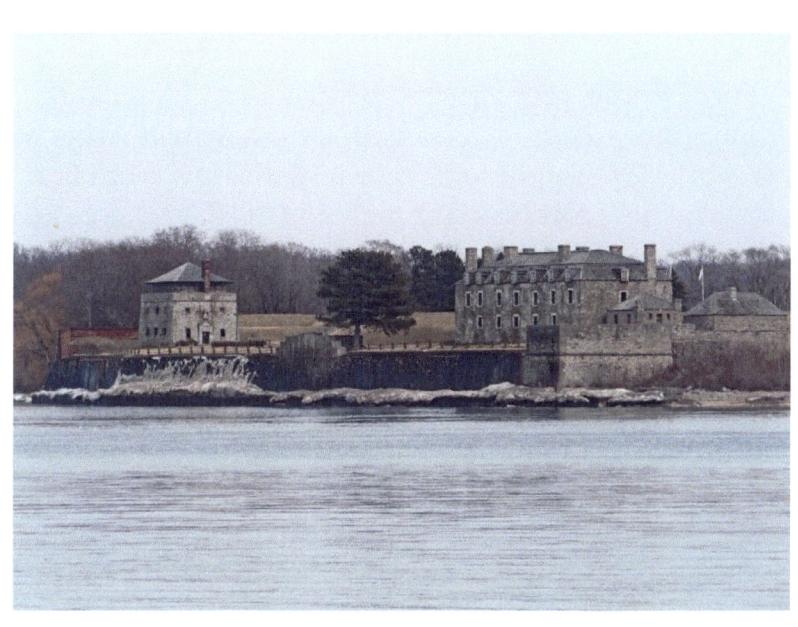

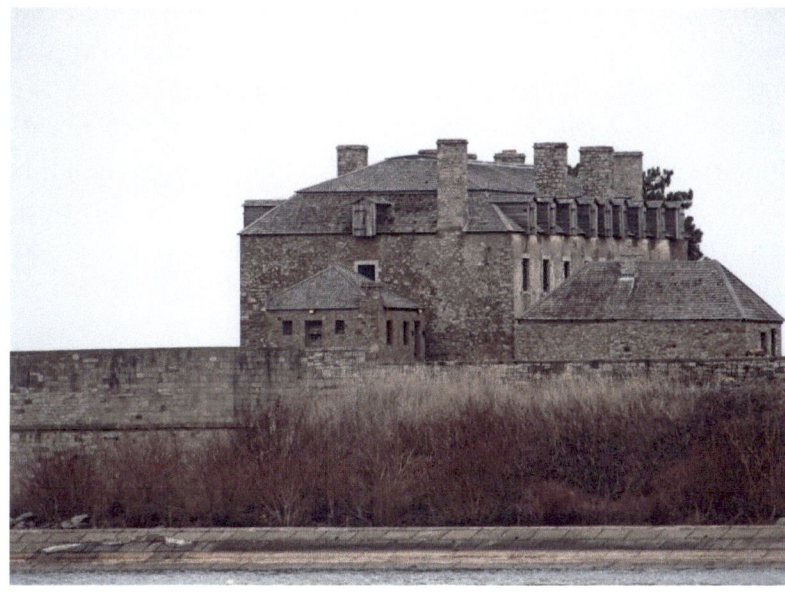

Fort George

Fort George, cconstructed by order of Lieutenant-Governor Simcoe 1796-99, was built by the British Army after Jay's Treaty (1796) required Britain to withdraw from Fort Niagara. The new fort was completed in 1802, and consisted of earthworks and palisades, along with internal structures, including an officer's quarters, blockhouses to accommodate other ranks and their families, and a stone powder magazine, which is the only original building on the site.

Fort George served as the headquarters for Major-General Brock in 1812. In May 1813 it was bombarded for two days by the American fleet and the batteries at Fort Niagara across the river. The British and Canadians, together with Aboriginal peoples allied with them, fought to oppose an American landing on Lake Ontario.

Fearing that the lighthouse might be filled with explosives, on the 27th a large American force was landed near Two Mile Creek, several miles to the west. An artillery battery manned by Canadian militia was located near this spot during the battle. It was overwhelmed by cannon fire from two U.S. vessels, the U.S. Julia, and the U.S. Growler, at point-blank range. After a brief engagement at Fort George in which his outnumbered garrison sustained heavy casualties, Brigadier-General John Vincent made an orderly withdrawal towards Burlington Heights.

The Americans constructed fortifications of their own on the site. The American Army used the fort as a base to invade Upper Canada. The capture of Fort George left the Americans in control of the Niagara frontier, but Vincent's troops a week later repelled the Americans at the Battles of Stoney Creek and Beaver Dams, preventing the Americans from gaining the whole peninsula. The U.S. forces were pinned down in Newark which they burned and abandoned on December 10, 1813 and Fort George was retaken by the British. In 1815, Fort George was described as "tumbling into ruins" and ordered abandoned. The present works are a reconstruction done in 1937-40, and represent the fort as it was in 1799-1813.

Butler's barracks complex was built out of range of U.S. artillery and it was used until 1824.

The fortification was used by the Canadian Army as a military training base during the First World War and through the Second World War under the name Camp Niagara. The grounds were abandoned by the military in 1965.

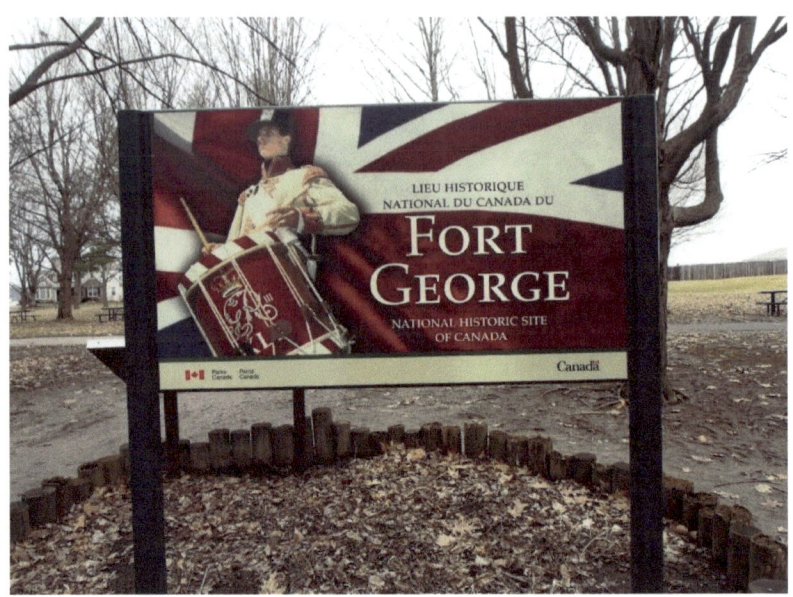

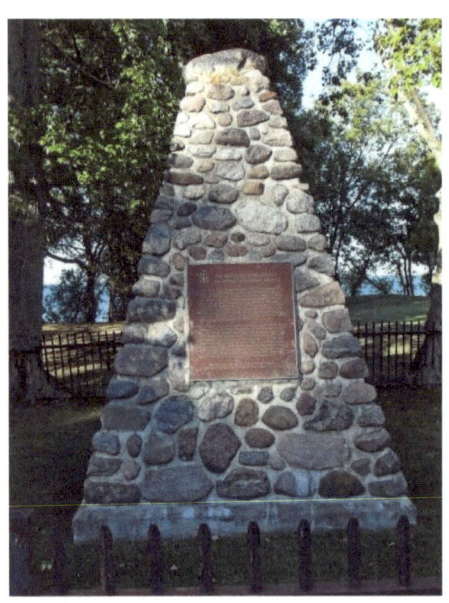

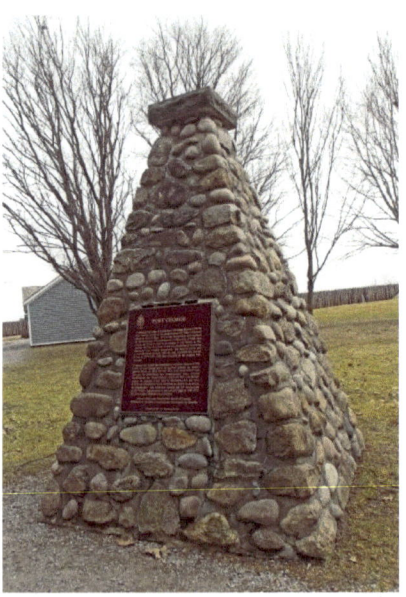

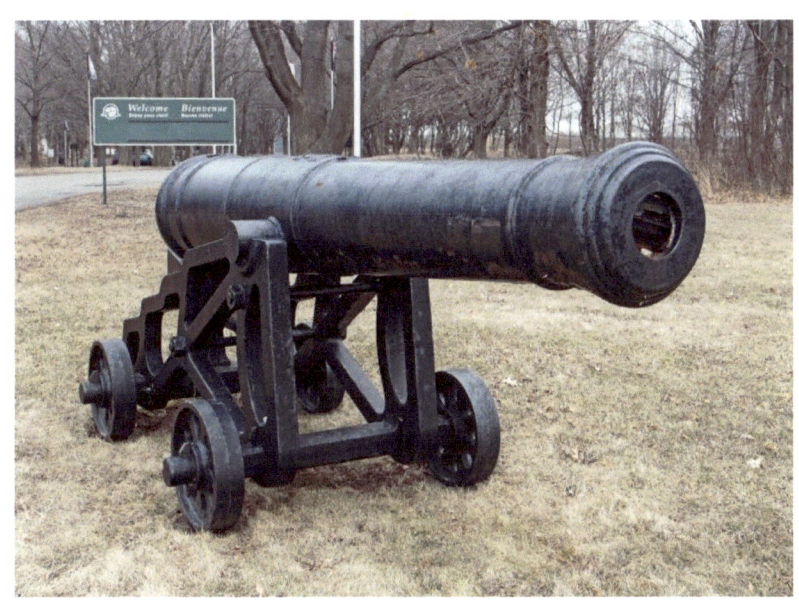

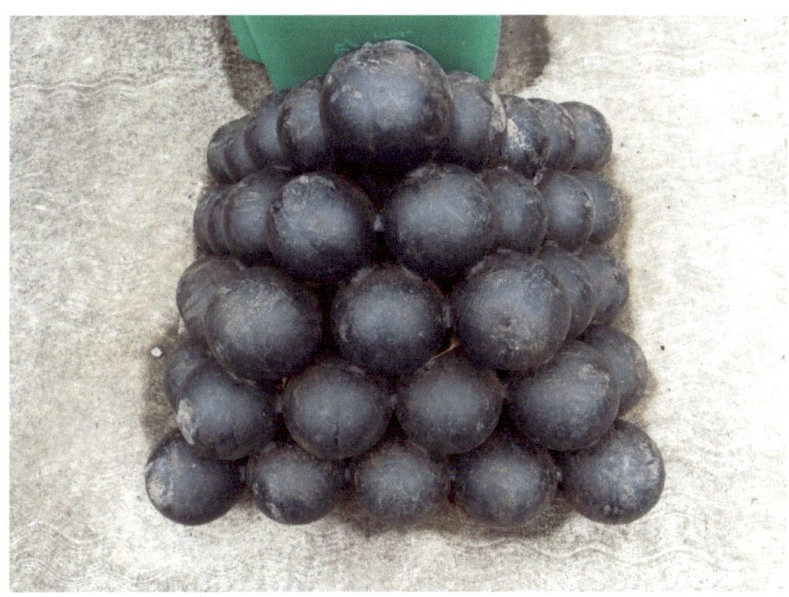

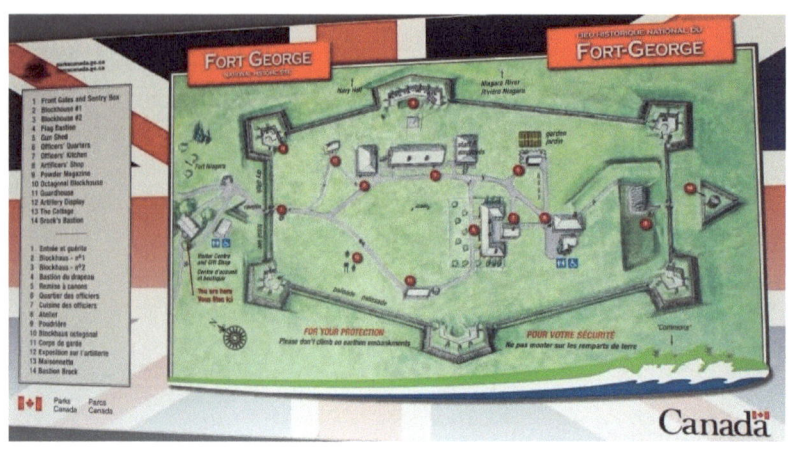

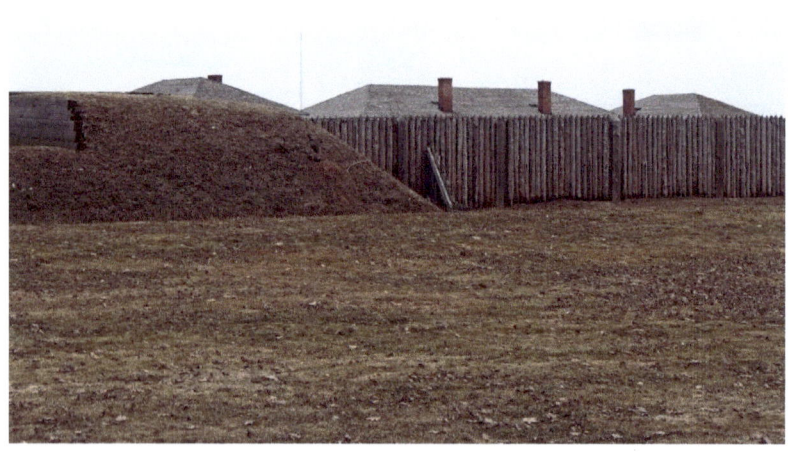

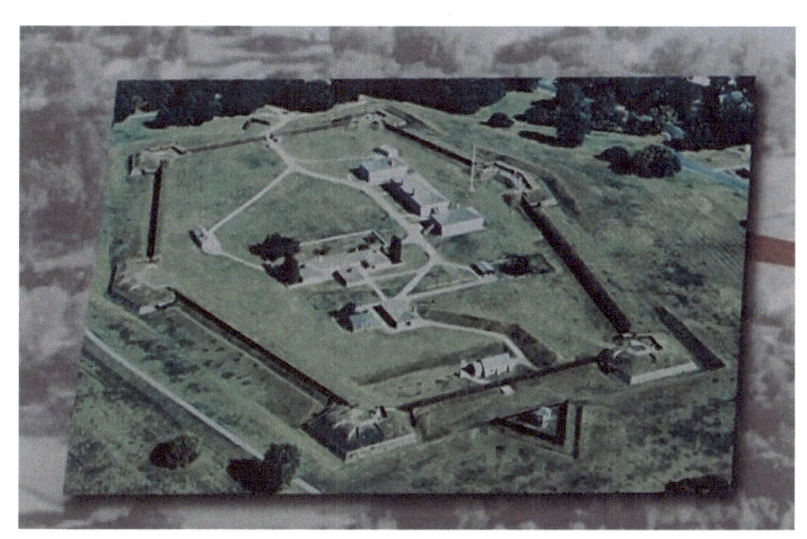

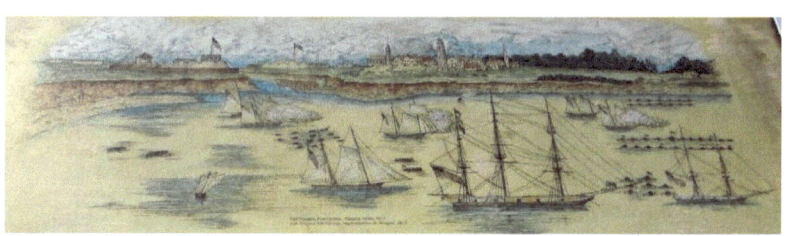

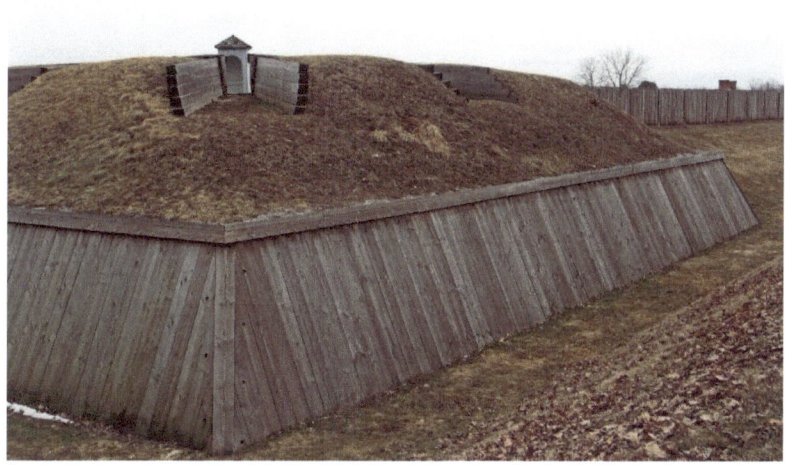

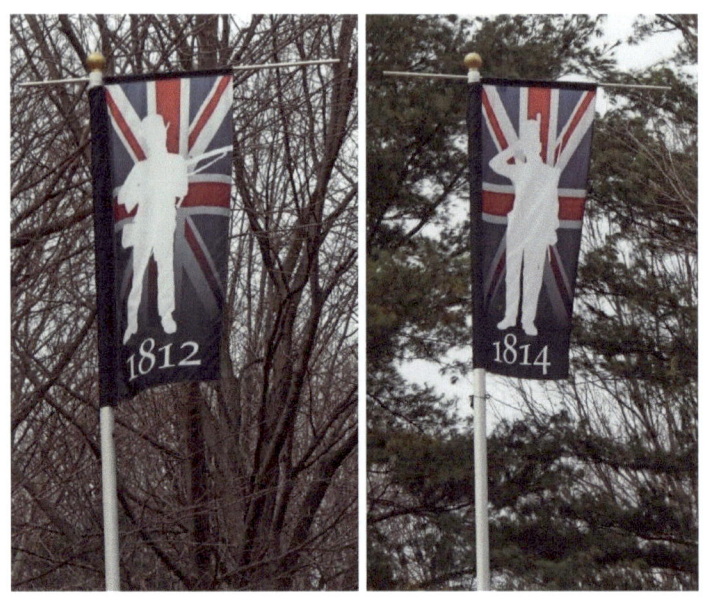

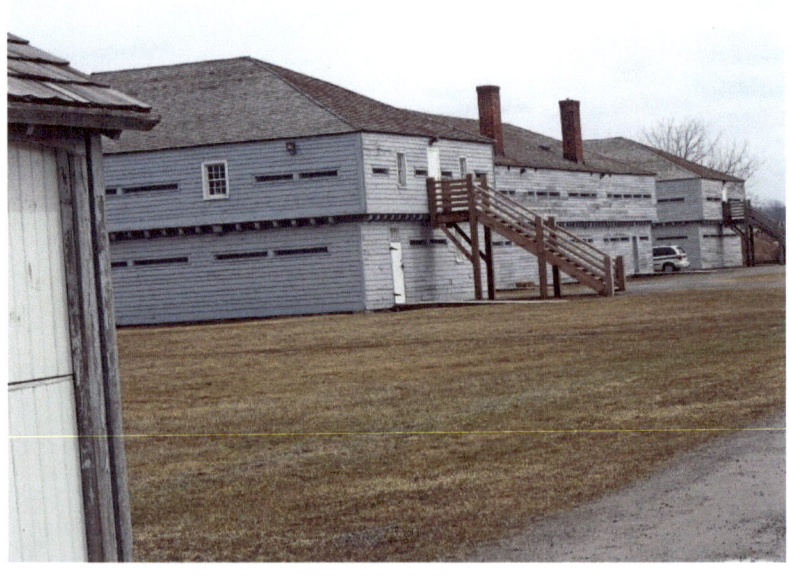

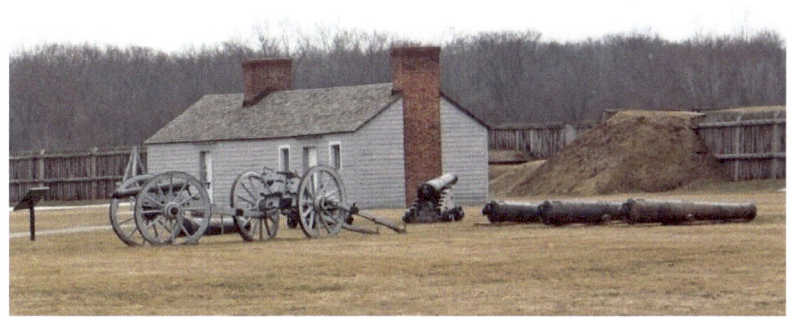

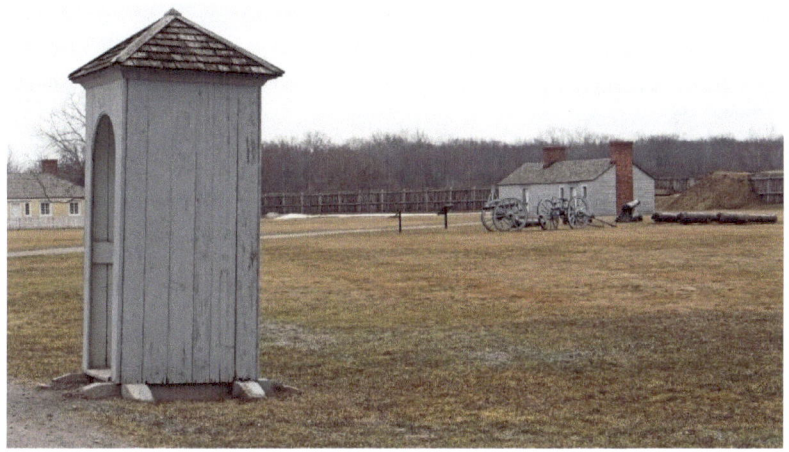

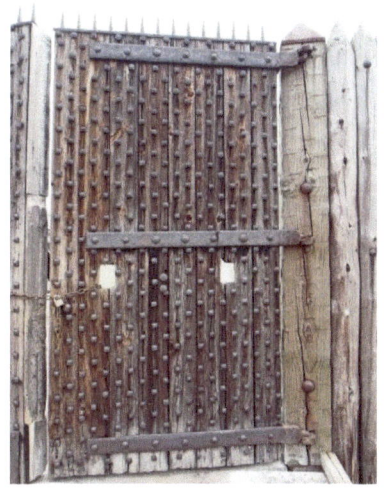

Fort Mississauga

Mississauga Point is located where the Niagara River flows into Lake Ontario. Lakes and rivers were military supply and transportation routes and forts were built to protect them.

After the British captured Fort Niagara on December 19, 1813, a new fort was constructed on the Canadian shore, called Fort Mississauga. Materials for it were obtained from the ruins of the nearby town of Newark (now Niagara-on-the-Lake). With the American navy now controlling Lake Ontario, this work was crucial to the security of British forces in the Niagara Peninsula.

Before the fort was built, the site was used by at least three Native American tribes: the Neutral (15th century); Seneca (late 17th century); and Mississauga (18th century). As early as 1790, Mississauga Point had been identified as a location for a fort. Plans date from 1799 for a battery of fourteen cannons to oppose Fort Niagara. In 1804, instead of a fort a lighthouse was erected at Mississauga Point; this was the first lighthouse on the Great Lakes. Fort George was built farther upstream.

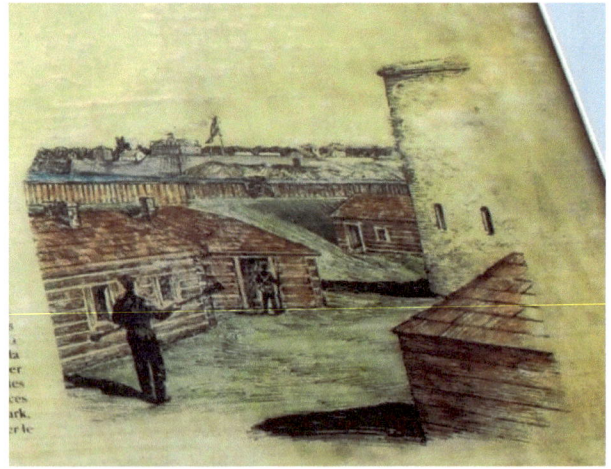

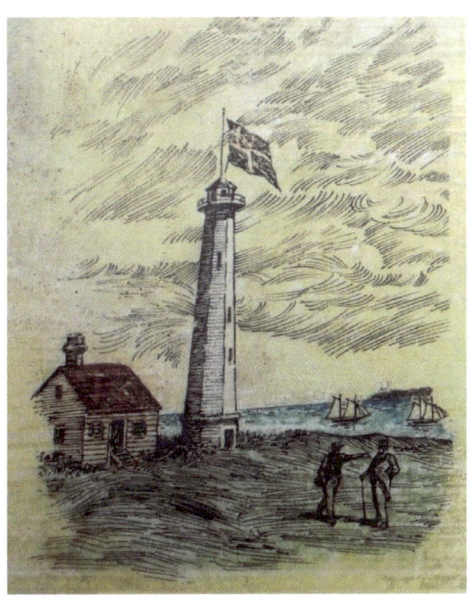

The lighthouse was dismantled in 1814 to make way for Fort Mississauga, which incorporated stone from the lighthouse in its construction. It was built on the remains of the first capital of Upper Canada.

The British Army was stationed at the fort from 1813 to 1855, followed by the Canadian Army, which used it as summer training ground beginning in the 1870s, then during both World Wars and the Korean War. A golf course was laid out nearby in the late 1870s. Today, Niagara-on-the-Lake Golf Course surrounds the site, but public access is permitted via a walking path, with a warning to look out for golfers, who have the right of way. The path starts at the corner of Front and Simcoe streets.

The block house is the only building of the original fort to survive with all other buildings destroyed or dismantled.

The interior of the blockhouse is closed, but has wooden staircases leading to some upper windows. The tower was completed in 1825 and measures 50' by 50'. The walls are 25' high, 8' thick at the base and slope slightly to 7' at the parapet. The walls are pierced with ventilation shafts on the ground floor and windows on the main floor. Inside, the basement contained two rooms, a storehouse and a gunpowder magazine. Ceilings are arched to provide extra protection under a bombardment. The main floor was also divided into two rooms designed as a barracks or living space for about 34 men. The wives and children of soldiers also lived here after the War of 1812.

The tower was planned as a barrack, an artillery battery, and a place of refuge and best defense under attack. Only a determined enemy with heavy cannon could hope to overpower it. The star-shaped fortification was intended to provide additional protection at the mouth of the Niagara River. Star-shaped earthworks were simple and took little time to build. It counter balanced Fort Niagara on the American shore opposite. After the Americans burned the town of Newark in 1813, the British tore down the remaining brick walls and chimneys to provide a foundation.

The tower was only two feet high in July when an American force under General Jacob Brown tested the defences of the fort. Soldiers stationed here during the war lived in log buildings inside the fort walls. In 1814 the walls were twenty feet thick to protect the defenders. Soldiers lining the ramparts could destroy an attacking force in the crossfire created by the angles of the star shape. It was difficult to defend since soldiers had to be stationed in every angle, unlike more common bastioned forts such as Fort George where troops only had to defend projecting bastions located at the corners of the fort.

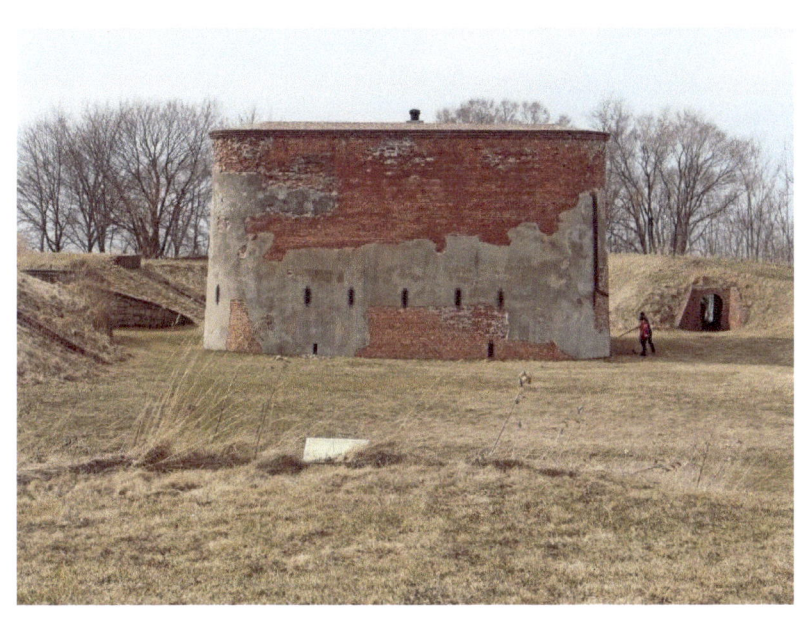

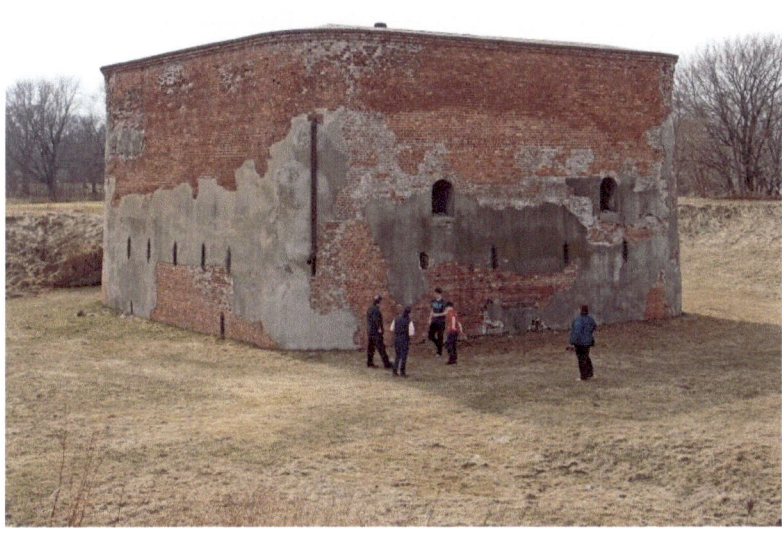

The Tower

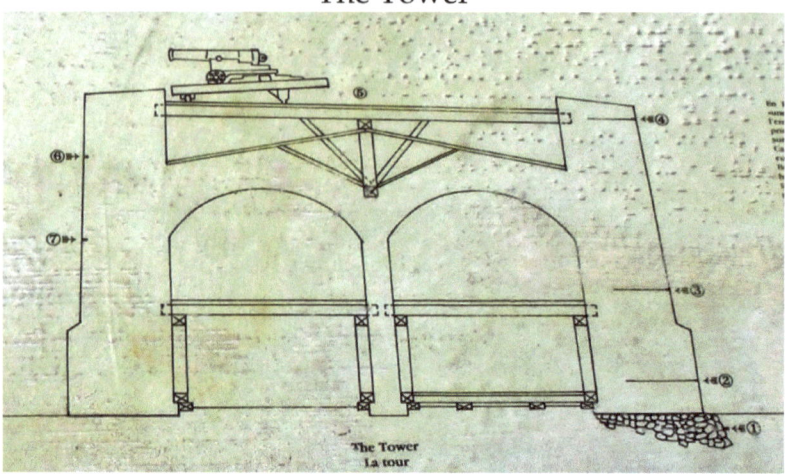

The Tower
La tour

1. Rubble from the 1792 town of Newark was place in 1814
2. July 1814 Americans attack the tower which is only two feet high
3. April 1816 the tower is nine feet high
4. 1823 – the tower is substantially complete
5. 1838 – upper batter for artillery is installed
6. 1840s – stucco parging applied to protect the brickwork
7. World War I soldiers apply concrete parging

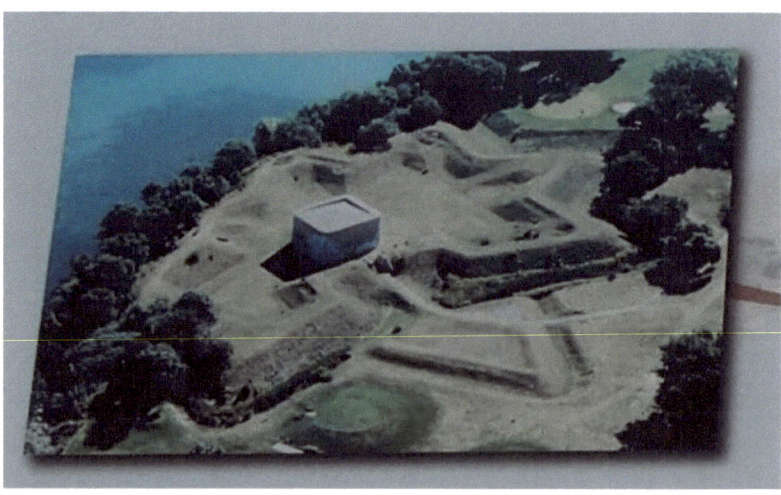

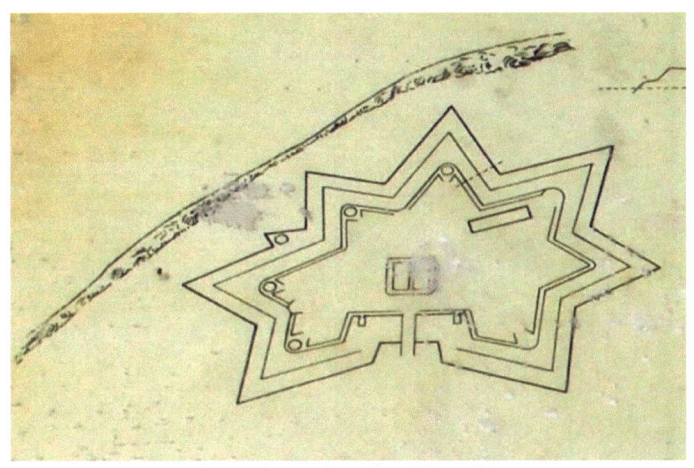

Plan dated July 29, 1814

The Fort That Never Was

At the end of the War of 1812 (in 1815), it was decided that a permanent fort for 1,000 men would be constructed here to replace Fort George which was in very poor condition. The new fort was to be ten times the size of the present one. Approved in concept, this could have become one of the largest forts in Canada. The lack of funding, change of Imperial priorities, and the development of more powerful weapons meant that no work was ever done. The importance of the waterway was reduced by the construction of Erie (1825) and Welland (1829) canals.

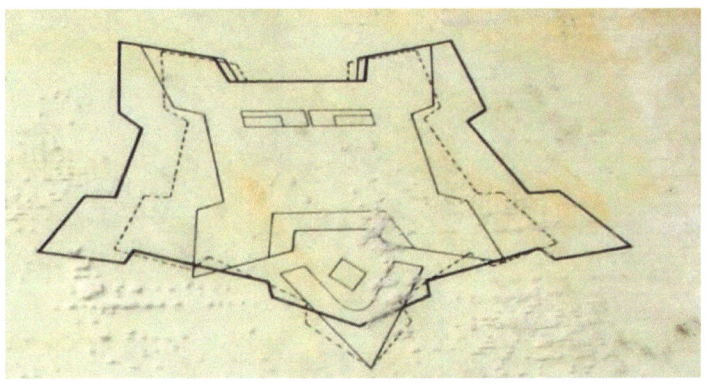

Fort Mississauga was a base for British/Canadian defence during the rebellion crisis in 1837. In the aftermath of the 1837-38 rebellions in Upper and Lower Canada, there was a flurry of military constructions in the colonies. The earthworks were now 40' thick and 12' high. A v-shaped earthwork called a ravelin protected the main gate. Two wooden bridges led into the fort. One of these was a drawbridge and could be raised. A double row of spiked logs protected the fort. The inner row of logs was placed vertically, with the outer row set into the ground at a forty-five degree angle, facing the enemy. Over a dozen cannons were placed in the fort.

In the 1840s, stucco parging was applied to the tower to protect the brickwork. It was a base for British/Canadian defence during U.S. Civil War and the Fenian Raids (1866 and 1870). World War I soldiers put concrete parging on the tower's exterior.

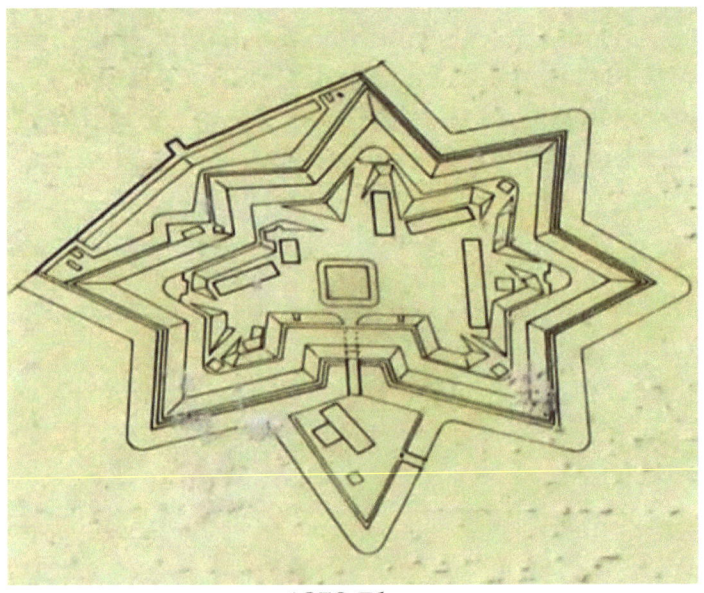

1852 Plan

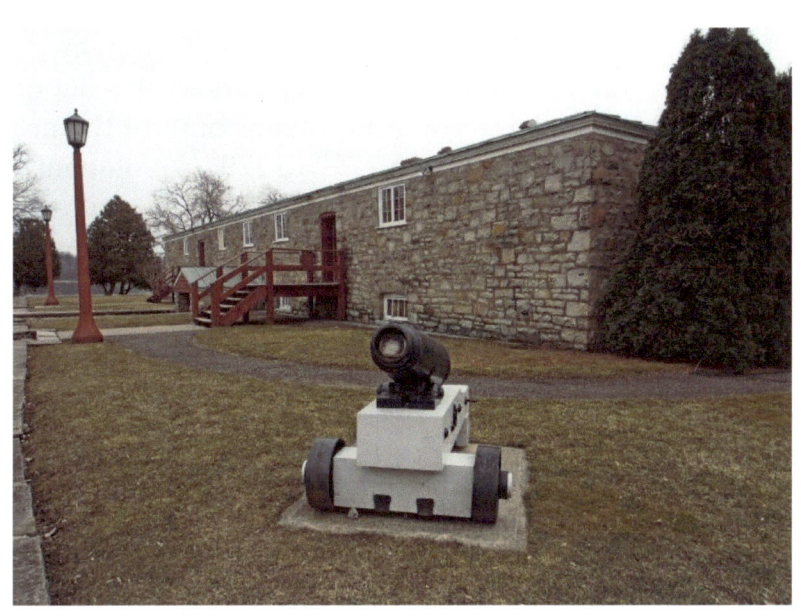

305 Ricardo Street – Navy Hall

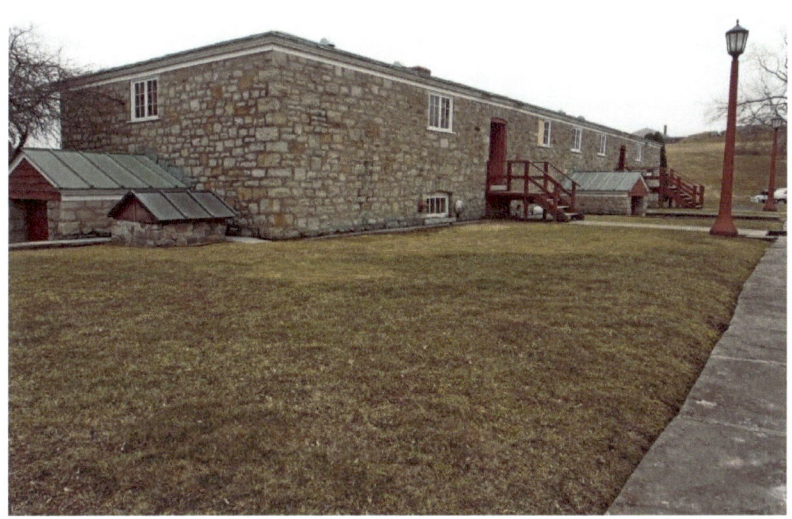

Navy Hall originally consisted of a small shipyard, storehouses, residences and docks which served as a depot for supplies; it also served as a transshipment point for the posts on the Upper Great Lakes. From 1792 to 1796, Lieutenant-Governor John Graves Simcoe had offices and his residence in the complex. These buildings were later converted to military use until destroyed by American artillery fire during the War of 1812.

Immediately after the War of 1812, a new wooden military storehouse was built on this site. It was converted into barracks for British troops during the border troubles of 1838. The building remained in use into the twentieth century, serving as a medical dispensary for Canadian troops during World War I. During the 1930s the building was moved to its present location and encased in stone.

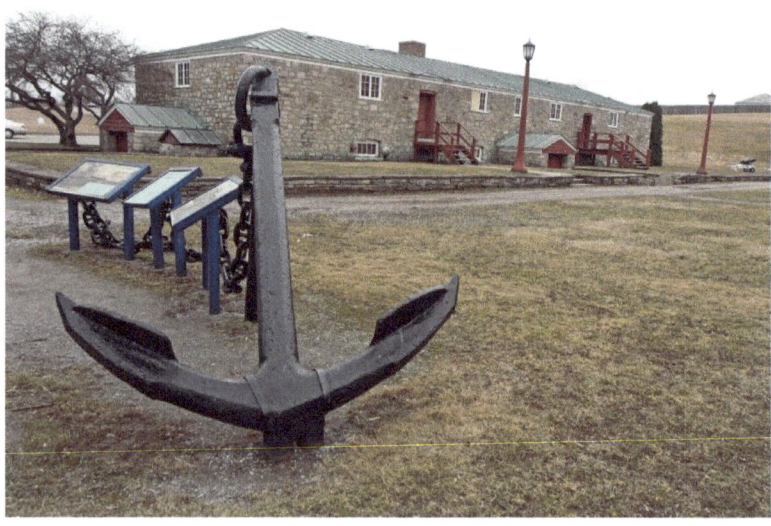

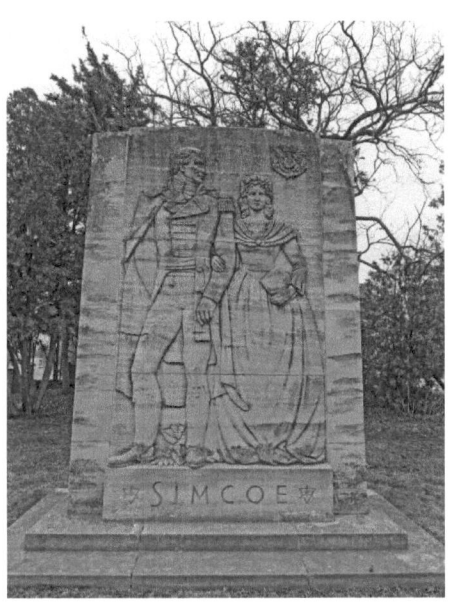

John Graves Simcoe was born in Northamptonshire in 1752 and educated at Oxford. He joined the British army in 1771 and from 1777-1781, he commanded the Queen's Rangers, a Loyalist corps in America. After the Loyalist influx had led to the creation of a separate province of Upper Canada in 1791, Simcoe was named its first Lieutenant-Governor. During his five years of office, the province's basically British and monarchical character and institutions took shape. After he left Canada in 1796, he held a succession of military and colonial offices, and died in Exeter in 1806 shortly after being appointed Commander-in-chief for India.

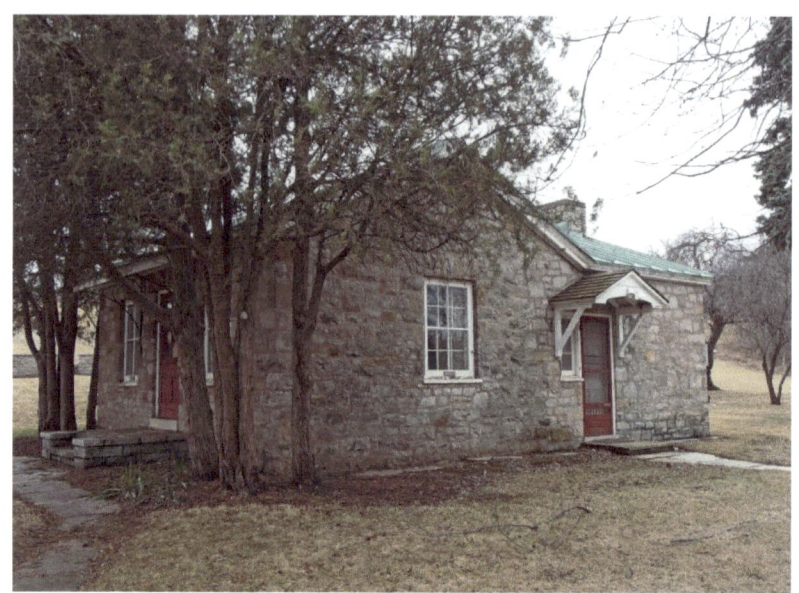

Ricardo Street

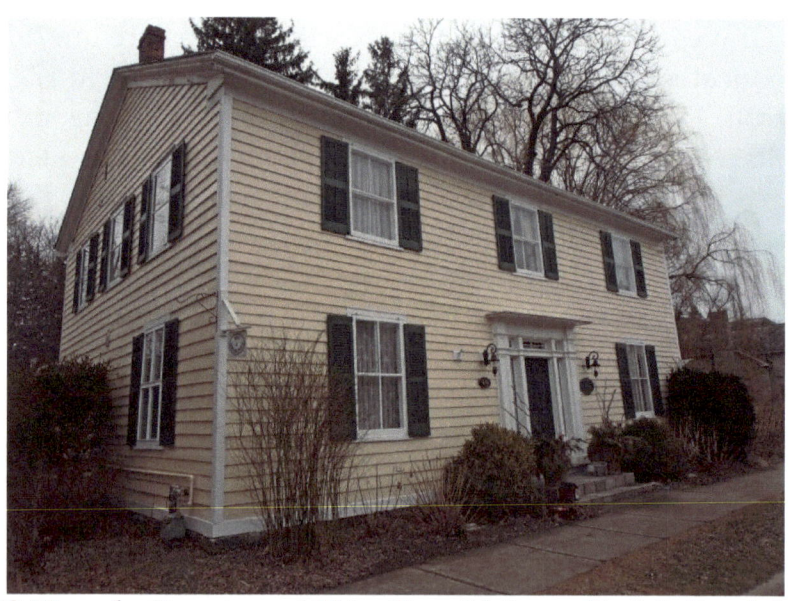

242 Ricardo Street – c. 1824 – Royal Manor Bed & Breakfast
Georgian style

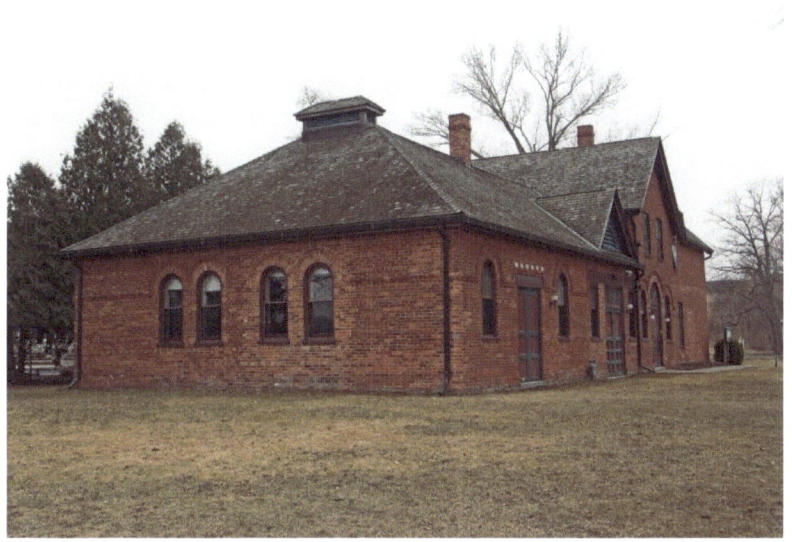

247 Ricardo Street – The Waterworks Pump House

The Waterworks Pump House was built in 1891 and served as a pumping station that supplied the town with water from the Niagara River until 1983. The original building contained a steam engine, water pumps, and a boiler with a 75 foot chimney. The building was constructed of brick and shows an asymmetrical composition of Romanesque character. In 1994 the exterior was restored to its original appearance; and interior renovations were designed to accommodate the Niagara Pump House Visual Art Centre.

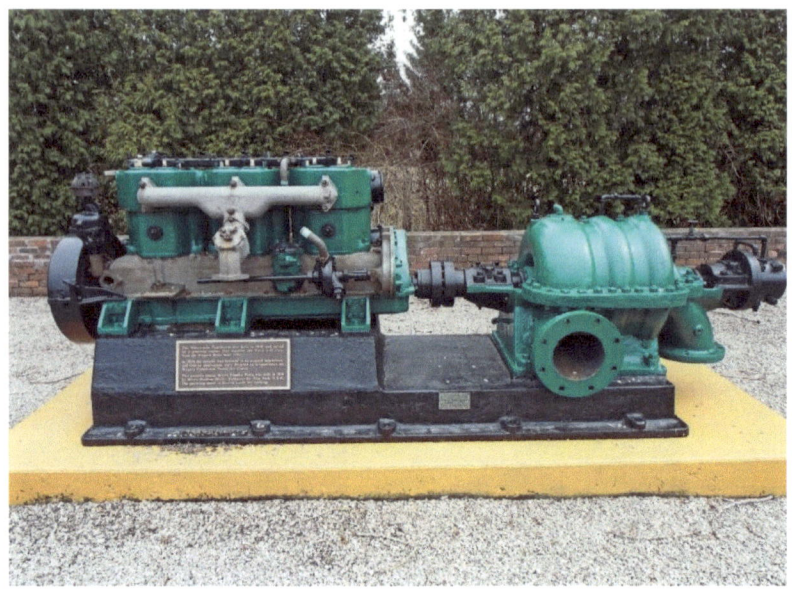

This gasoline engine standby pump was built in 1919 by Morris Machine Works, Baldwinsville, New York, U.S.A. The operating panel is located inside the building.

The Niagara Harbour and Dock Company, formed by local businessmen in 1831, created a shipping basin on the Niagara River by hiring hundreds of labourers to excavate a riverside marsh. By the late 1830s, the company employed about 400 workers and operated a busy port and shipyard in Upper Canada. The company's industrial complex was used to build railway cars and steamboats in the 1850s and 1860s.

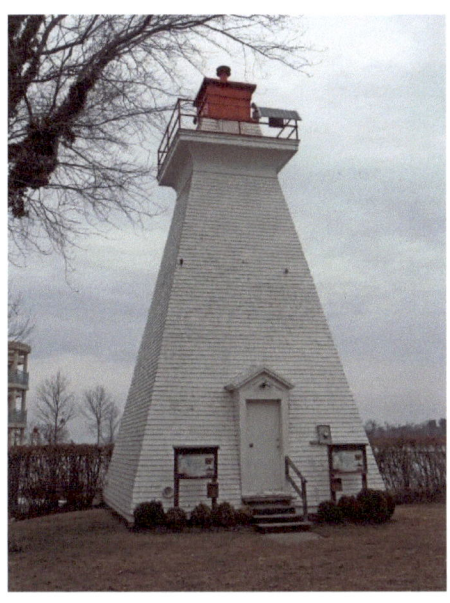

This lighthouse, operated by Canada Coast Guard – Fisheries and Oceans, is one of two marking the entrance to the Niagara River. The pyramid-shaped tower of this rear range light is 45 feet tall with a red-orange, electrically equipped lantern room on top. The front range light, located at the marina downstream, is identical but about 15 feet lower. Both lights were established in 1903 and are still in use today as shipping navigation aids.

Environment Canada has operated a sampling site at Niagara-on-the-Lake since 1975 to monitor the water quality of the Niagara River. In 1988 field and laboratory sampling equipment were installed in this lighthouse. Submersible pumps located in a wet well beneath the gazebo supply the lighthouse laboratory with a 24-hour bi-weekly water sample from the river.

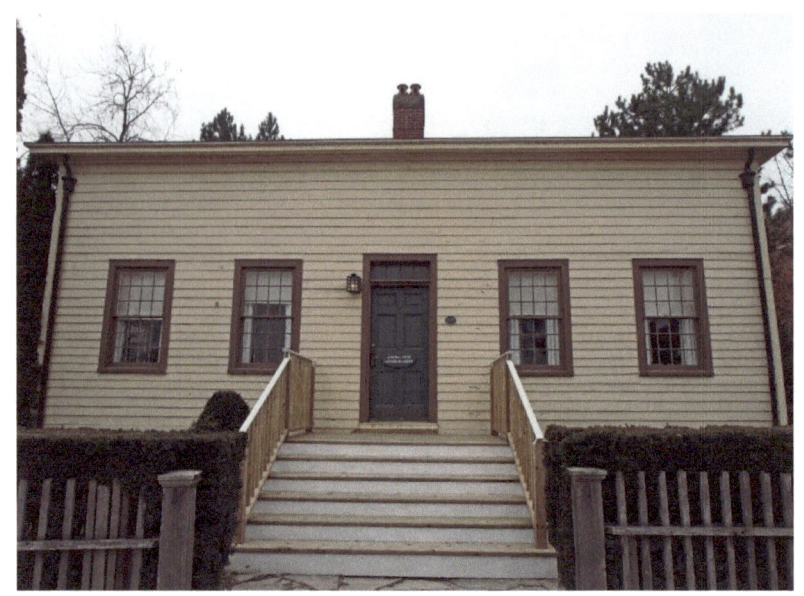

Ricardo Street – Admiral Suite, Sovereign Suite

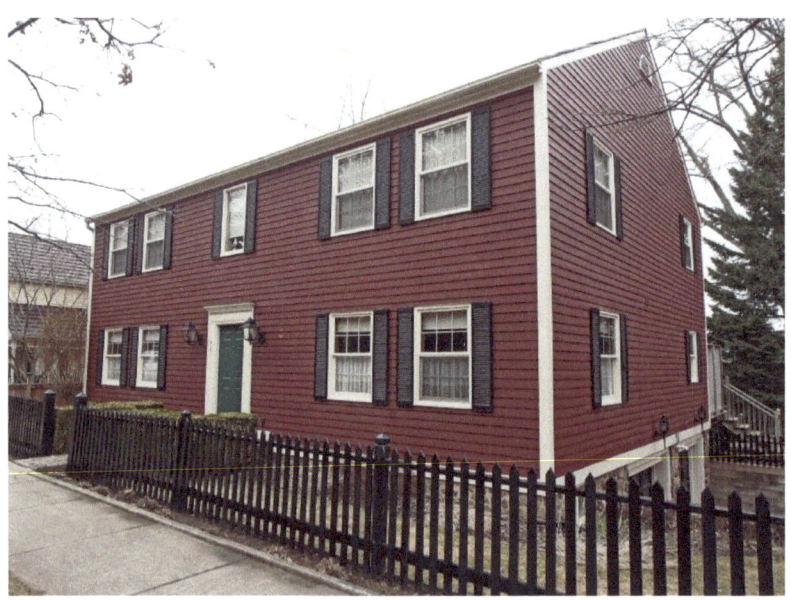

75 Ricardo Street – Georgian

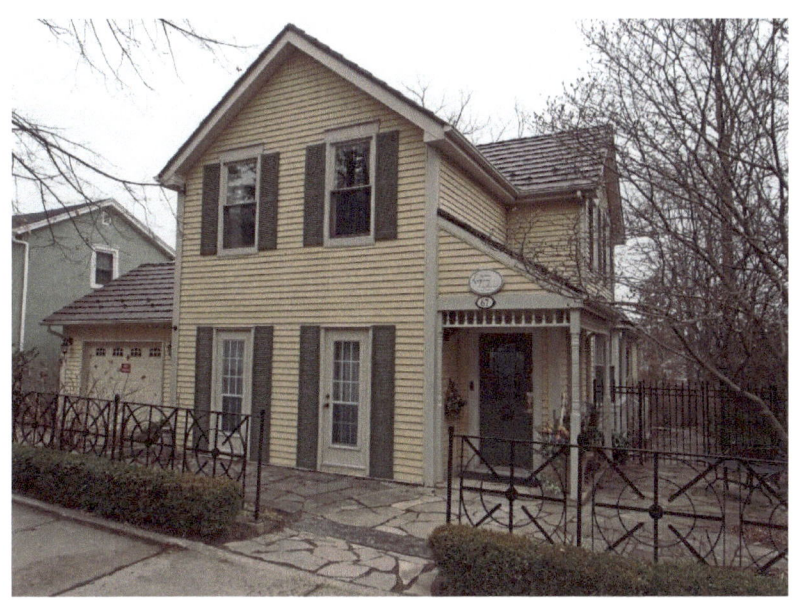

Gothic Revival

67 Ricardo Street - Andrew Logan House c. 1860

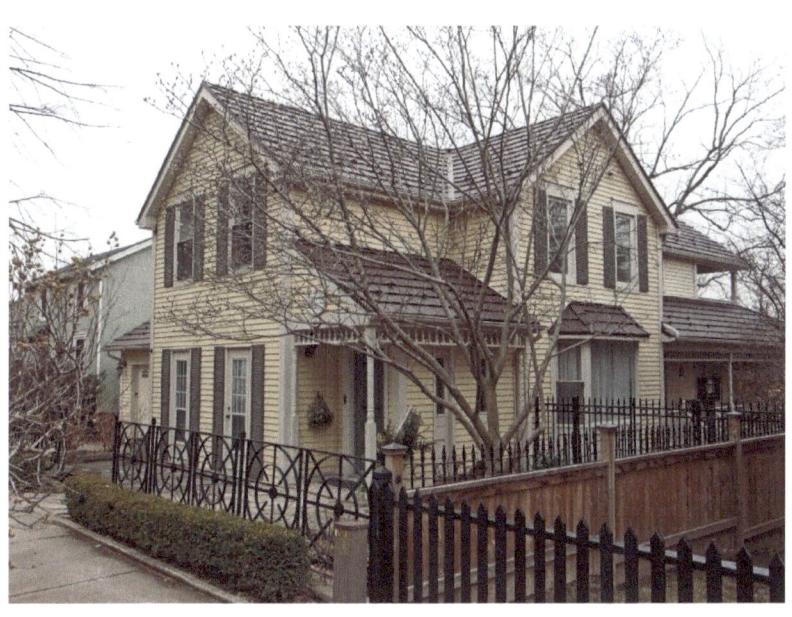

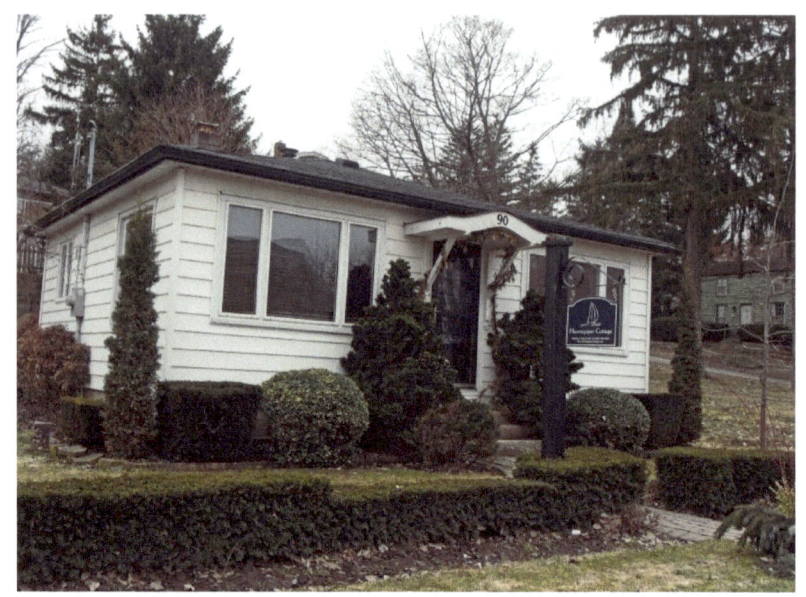

90 Ricardo Street

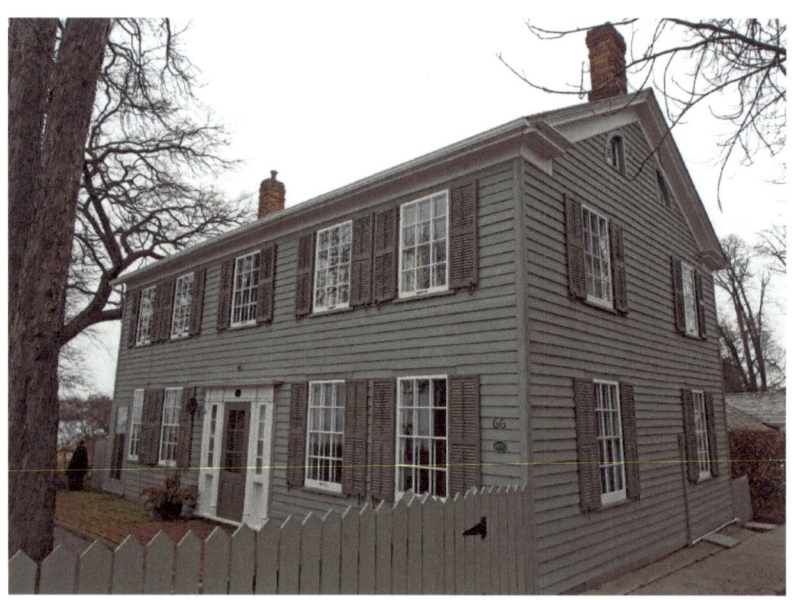

66 Ricardo Street – c. 1835 – Georgian style

The Upper Canada Gazette, or American Oracle, the first newspaper in what is now Ontario was produced in the town of Niagara with its first issue dated April 18, 1793. *The Gleaner*, one of the most prominent newspapers in Upper Canada, was produced here from 1817-1837.

On June 8, 1800, the Niagara Library, the first circulating library in Upper Canada, was established. Some 80 works were available for circulation, many on religion and history. The collection was steadily enlarged.

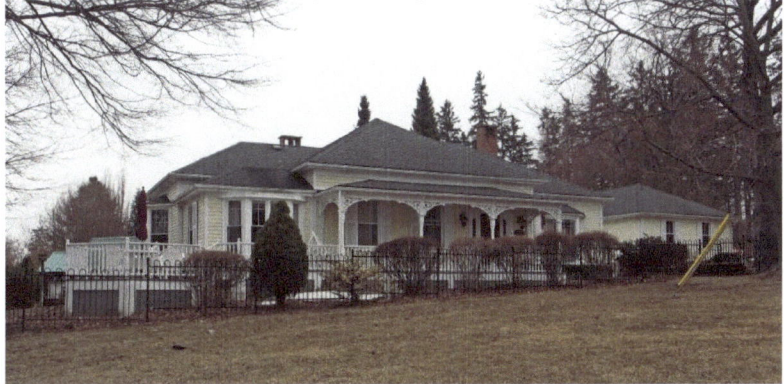

Ricardo Street – Arbour View c. 1900

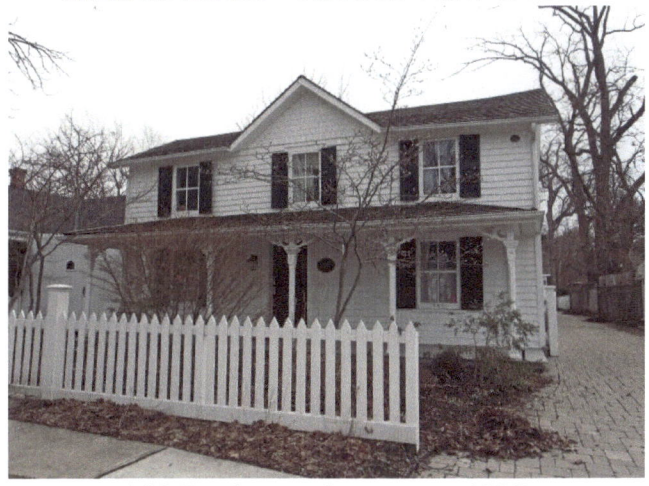

132 Prideaux Street – c. 1832

Building Styles

Georgian, before 1860 – This style began with the British King Georges in the 18th century. These buildings have balanced facades around a central door, medium-pitched gable roofs, and small paned windows. Example: 66 Ricardo Street, see Page 34	
Gothic Revival, 1830-1890 – These decorative buildings have sharply-pitched gables with highly detailed verge boards, pointed-arch window openings, and dichromatic brickwork. It is a common style in Ontario. Example: 67 Ricardo Street	
Romanesque Revival, 1880-1910 – This style hearkens back to medieval architecture of the 11th and 12th centuries with a heavy appearance, blocky towers and rounded arches. Example: Pump House, Ricardo Street	

www.ingramcontent.com/pod-product-compliance
Lightning Source LLC
Chambersburg PA
CBHW041150180526
45159CB00002BB/767

*9 7 8 1 5 1 4 1 6 3 8 3 2 *